Guillotined

Being a Summary Broadside Against the Corruption of the English Language

Alexander Cockburn

and the Readers of CounterPunch

First published by CounterPunch 2012

CounterPunch
PO Box 228
Petrolia, California
95558

ISBN 978-0-615-68956-2

A catalog record for this book is available
from the Library of Congress.

Library of Congress Control Number: 2012948031

Edited by Jeffrey St. Clair

Design and typography by
Tiffany Wardle de Sousa

Typeset in Minion Pro, designed by Robert Slimbach for Adobe Systems Inc., P22 Operina Pro designed by Ludovico degli Arrighi and James Grieshaber for IHOF, and P22 1722 designed by Ted Staunton for P22 type foundry/Sherwood Type.

Printed and bound in the U.S.A.

It's early morning on a spring day in the month of Praireal, Year of the Revolution II in Paris. But already the tricoteuses are making sure they have their seats in front of the guillotine in the Place de la Revolution.

Rumor is running rife. Prosecutor Fouquier-Tinville has agreed that there are certain words which have counter-revolutionary potential, in the sense they have the power, as Fouquier put it, to debase and coarsen common speech by repeated and thoughtless use.

There's a grinding noise, a squeaking of axle and round the corner from its long journey from the Conciergerie comes the first load of the condemned.

¶ First up: "sustainable." It's been at least a quarter of a century since this earnest word was drained of all energy, having become the prime unit of exchange in the argot of purposeful uplift by non-profit organizations. It was Gro Bruntland in 1987 who laid the curse on common diction of "sustainable development." These days fund-raisers and grant-writers string it round each sentence like an adjectival fannypack, bulging with self-congratulation. Mostly, the term is meaningless or a vague expression of hope. As the final indication of its degraded status, I found it in President Obama's "signing statement," which accompanied the whisper of his pen, as on New Year's Eve — a very quiet day when news editors were all asleep — he signed into law the National Defense Authorization Act (NDAA) for 2012 which handed $662 billion to the Pentagon and for good measure ratified by legal statute the exposure of US citizens to arbitrary arrest without subsequent benefit of counsel, and to possible torture and imprisonment sine die, abolishing habeas corpus. Don't bother to ask what happens to non-US citizens.

As he set his name to this repugnant legislation the president issued a "signing statement" in which I came upon the following passage: "Over the last several years, my Administration has developed an effective, sustainable framework for the detention, interrogation and trial of suspected terrorists..."

So much for "sustainable." Into the tumbrils with it.

¶ Tumbril Time! A tumbril (n.) a dung cart used for carrying manure, now associated with the transport of prisoners to the guillotine during the French Revolution.

¶ Next up: "iconic." I trip over this golly-gee epithet thirty times a day. No warrant for its arrest is necessary, nor benefit of counsel or trial in a US court. Off to the tumbrils, arm in arm with "narrative."

¶ I think "parse" has almost run its course, though occasionally this shooting star of 2011 is still to be spotted panting along in some peloton of waffle from the Commentariat. Off with its head, along with "meme," an exhausted little word that deserves the long dark rest of oblivion.

¶ The Conciergerie is at the west end of the Ile de la Cite where the cathedral of Notre Dame stands. Part of the Palais de Justice, it was where suspects were famously taken during the French Revolution. In the early years following the fall of the Bastille in 1789, you had a sporting chance of walking out of the Conciergerie with head and shoulders still connected. A notice on the stone wall next to a bust of Robespierre said that in the Revolution's first year only a third of the accused were found guilty. The pace really picked up after the establishment in the spring of 1793 of the Revolutionary Tribunal and the installation of public prosecutor Antoine Fouquier-Tinville, who bustled well over a thousand into eternal sleep ("Death is nothing but eternal sleep" was posted in all cemeteries of the revolutionary period), including Marie Antoinette, Danton, Hebert and Robespierre, before the blade fell on Fourquier's own neck in May 1795. His trial lasted forty-one days and he said he was only a lawyer doing his job and why didn't they go after the guys who gave him the job.

These days the Disneyfication of historical sites proceeds in lockstep with the construction of those worldwide boondoggles par excellence, "visitor centers" and "heritage" facilities. Not so in the Conciergerie, a heavy place. You can imagine being hauled there, dumped in a cell along with a passel of Viscomtes and Ducs, given your minute in court and not long thereafter taken to the door — there it was right in front of my nose — behind which was a horse harnessed to the tumbril, with Madam Defarge and her knitting crew waiting for you in the front row. This is where the guillotine stood in what is now the Place de la Concorde, near the Crillon Bar.

¶ Fred Gardner writes: "Add 'Gamechanger' to the mis- and over-used words of 2011. For years I've winced as lawyers and businessmen and reporters casually used 'game' in reference to the legal system, finance, war itself... You sometimes see a bumper sticker on a sports car that says 'the one with the most toys wins.' It makes me want to give them a little nudge with the old Volvo..."

¶ Jon Swift: "Also the drug-treatment shibboleth: 'The user's always chasing that first high.' As though they couldn't *possibly* enjoy it the 875th time. You never hear 'Religious worshippers are always chasing that first feeling of being at one with God' or 'Voters are always chasing that first thrill they got on entering the booth at 18....'"

¶ Wat Stearns: "I nominate 'expensed' and 'leveraged' for the tumbrils as well."

¶ Let me toss in the odious "project," initially favored by the left but now in general currency, attached to almost every human endeavor. And let us note the meteoric rise of "existential."

¶ For three or four years now people have been having a "conversation." The word has come of age. I see it bowing and scraping on the opinion pages and TV talk shows three or four times a day. "National conversations" are clubby affairs. Their prime purpose is to exclude the unconversational, meaning intellectual or verbal excess; above all, unseemly questioning of the essential functionality of the existing system. Indeed, I began to keep an eye out for the term when I read a column in which some rabble-rouser was haughtily black-balled as most definitely not being part of the national conversation.

It's possible that the "national conversation" got its start as an effort to dignify the interactions of the "chattering classes," a phrase which had its origin as a right-wing snarl, in the Thatcher years. Real men and real women didn't chatter. They moved briskly forward with the business of "governance," yet another irksome locution.

¶ Now to the tumbrils with the equally annoying "if you will," beloved of Wolf Blitzer, John King and the other TV anchors and correspondents. "If you will" is something between a sheep-like cough and a verbal tail-wag, a signifier of decorum, itself a prime ingredient of the "national conversation." As noted, it's a particular favorite of the CNN crowd, and recommended to me for the blade by Leslie Cockburn. The phrase serves the function of a pre-emptive apology every time the reporter or commentator makes something approaching a substantive statement. The late Christopher Hitchens used it a lot, archly.

¶ Any headline modeled on "It's the economy, stupid." This tedious phrase derives from the Clinton campaign of 1992, and is still echoing on opinion pages 20 years on. To the tumbrils with it!

¶ "Well...," as in constructs like "His performance was... well... frankly bad." Equally awful is "...er," as in "Is Angeline Jolie a great actor? Er... no." The British are particularly keen on this piece of stylistic coyness.

¶ "Staunch," as so often used to describe right-wingers: "a staunch Republican," "a staunch Conservative," though not I think, "a staunch fascist." I see left writers using this phrase freely about Republicans and Conservatives. Don't they know that "staunch" carries the aroma of unstinting, courageous loyalty. It's an honorific. How about "fanatic Republican?" "crazed Conservative." No right-winger would talk about "staunch liberals"—admittedly an oxymoron, just like "staunch Democrat." Now, there really are staunch pacifists. Save the word for them.

¶ "At the end of the day," which, I need scarcely remind you, is the hour when the "fat lady sings," after the "rubber has met the road." The fat lady line was first popularized in George H.W. Bush's run for the Republican nomination in 1980. When he finally threw in the towel, the press corps hired a fat Valkyrie with a horned helmet to rush up to him and sing at the top of her voice, waving a trident.

¶ From Jean-Pierre Duboucheron: "Bad guys." Spot on, Jean-Pierre.

¶ From Sean Dunne in Ireland: "this ain't my first rodeo;" "just sayin;'" "Really." True, one does see the terse "Really," all too often. Time for the final haircut.

¶ "I would like to request that you consign one more word to the tumbrils. And that word is 'stakeholder.'" Vukoni Lupa-Lasaga. Happy to oblige, Vukoni.

¶ From Egidio Mondolfi: "Natalie Bauman and I submit 'folks' for your consideration. If ever a word was long overdue for a ride in the farm cart..."

¶ Recently the revolutionary Prosecutor Fouqier-Tinville announced the capture and imminent trial of "grow," long sought in its counter-revolutionary mutation as a transitive verb governing an abstraction, as in "grow the economy," a formulation popular among the Girondin faction. "Grow," said the Prosecutor, was being held in the Conciergerie, under constant surveillance.

I've no doubt that the Tribunal will not long delay in sending "grow" in this usage to a well-deserved rendez-vous with the fatal blade. I associate the usage with the 1992 Clinton campaign, where talk about "growing the economy" was at gale force. My friends and neighbors here in Petrolia, Karen and Joe Paff, tell me that when they were starting up their coffee business, Goldrush, at the start of the 1980s, the local bank officials were already hard at it, talking about "growing the business." I hate the usage, with its smarmy implication of virtuous horticultural effort. As CounterPuncher Michael Greenberg writes, "It sounds phony, aggressive, and even grammatically incorrect, not the nurturing 'grow' that one associates with living things."

¶ Joining "grow" in the tumbril will, I trust, be "blood and treasure," used with great solemnity by opinion formers to describe the cost, often the supposedly worthy sacrifice, attached to America's wars. The usage apparently goes back to Jefferson, but that's no excuse. The catch-phrase seeks to turn slaughter and the shoveling of money to arms manufacturers into a noble, almost mythic expenditure.

¶ Shackled to "blood and treasure" should be its co-conspirator, "in harm's way." Jack Flannigan writes from Kerala:

> Mr. Cockburn, somebody might have beat me to it but my candidate for the squeaky old tumbril is 'in harm's way.' It has, especially in the last ten years, acquired a treacly red, white and blue patina about it that is overwhelmingly connected to the military and police.
>
> Someone sailing on a Gaza flotilla or staring down a line of sneering, rabid cops is not very likely to be referred by our political/media elites as 'in harm's way.'

¶ Recently, dispatching the phrase to the tumbrils, I said the G. H.W Bush campaign of 1980 for the Republican nomination hefted "It's not over till the fat lady sings" to national prominence. Jeremy Pikser writes to say the phrase "was actually first popularized by the coach (or owner?) of the Baltimore Bullets basketball team in 1978. As usual Bush was only capable of feeble imitation when he used it, hoping to sound like a 'real guy.'" Further research discloses its use in sports journalism has been attributed to writer/broadcaster Dan Cook around the same time, and in the mid-70s by a Texas Tech sports official.

¶ These days everyone has a narrative, an earnest word originally recruited, I believe, by anthropologists. So we read "according to the Pentagon's narrative..." Why not use some more energetic formulation, like, "According to the patent nonsense minted by the Pentagon's press office...?"

Suddenly we're surrounded by "narratives," all endowed with equal status.

Here's a good example of its baneful penetration into the language, in a Reuter's news story: "Rubio initially cast himself as the U.S.-born son of Cuban immigrants who fled Fidel Castro's revolution in 1959. That narrative ran aground when records surfaced showing that his parents actually had left Cuba years earlier."

Rubio is caught telling a big lie, and it gets demurely tricked out as a "narrative."

¶ Fouquier also passed sentence on the hiccupping "well" construction. Here it is in the first paragraph of Paul Krugman's column for January 27. "Mitch Daniels, the former Bush budget director who is now Indiana's governor, made the Republicans' reply to President Obama's State of the Union address. His performance was, well, boring."

What's coy little "well" doing in that sentence?

¶ "Dear Alex, My nomination for tumbril baggage is 'It is what it is.' Way overused, and vacuous in any case. Thanks, Kathy."

¶ Kevin Rath writes:

> Mr. Cockburn, Recently I have been accosted with the phrase 'reaching out to you' by sales people. While it may be inappropriate since your focus is the news, this stupid phrase people from marketing use in their email

> subject titles and language is really annoying. Reaching out to your Tumbril cart, Kevin Rath, A CP member.

Thank you, Kevin.

¶ Quitting time in Afghanistan brings us back to "in harm's way"—a phrase usually occurring in the same paragraph as "blood and treasure," which went to the guillotine last week amid particularly delighted cackles from the tricoteuses knitting in the Place de la Révolution.

Among those pressing Prosecutor Fouquier-Tinville to haul "in harm's way" into the dock was my brother Patrick, who was also trying to shove "go-to person" into the tumbrils. I use this phrase from time to time and felt a twinge. Fortunately, Patrick changed his mind, writing to me,

> I have rather changed my mind on 'Go-to person.' 'Sejanus, becoming known as the go-to person in the court of Tiberius'—Easy to mock, but is there a word or phrase conveying the same idea? I am not sure there is and uncertain Fouquier-Tinville would have been wholly satisfied that it was a case for the tumbril.

¶ Denny Chericone advises that "For a good time if you haven't seen it before—*In Harm's Way* with The Duke, The Kirk, Henry Fonda, Patricia Neal, Franchot Tone, Franchot Tone!? All brought together by Otto Preminger. Worth a view because I've never seen a WW II movie shot in a bathtub before. Then you'll really be looking for that tumbril."

¶ I've learned once more that it is always dangerous—if you will—to make any statement regarding sports history. Last week I cited CounterPuncher Jeremy Pikser on the source for "it's not over till the fat lady sings." Pikser wrote to say the phrase "was actually first popularized by the coach (or owner?) of the Baltimore Bullets basketball team in 1978." James Blum promptly wrote that "your source on the Fat Lady was wrong in a detail, the NBA champion Bullets of Wes Unseld and Elvin Hayes were in Washington in 1978." (Blum, thirsty for blood, added, "May I nominate for the tumbrils the pomo-prog 'excavate' and 'unpack?'"

And then there's this qualification from Richard Stack:

> Alex, just a note on the actual origin of "It's not over till the fat lady sings." It is a line in an old 1930/40 movie with Wallace Beery and Jackie Coogan. The two of them

> are improbably at an opera. The kid says "When can we leave?" Beery says "Not till it's over" The kid says "When will be over?" Beery says, "It ain't over till the fat lady sings."

¶ It's time for clôture on "closure," beloved of American families mustered in front of prisons on execution day. It's an odious word, fragrant with fake feeling, with the cold breath of an undertaker lowering the coffin lid. Prosecutor Fouquier-Tinville is mustering the necessary documentation and witnesses with his usual scrupulous attention to the rights of the accused.

¶ This just in from Doug Lummis in Okinawa:

> Alex, the bottom line is, to the tumbril with 'the bottom line.' I think it was about 15 or 20 years ago, suddenly everybody was talking about 'the bottom line.' I asked around, the bottom line to what? Nobody seemed to know. On the bottom line of a letter is the signature. On the bottom line of an invoice is how much you owe. In fishing, I suppose a bottom line will be good for catching bottom fish. In the language of seduction, presumably the bottom line will be something obscene. In comedy, it would be the punch line. But in politics there is no bottom line, because there's always the next page. Doug Lummis

¶ Back in the 1960s Herbert Marcuse pointed out in one of his books that the Pentagon had given up on verbs. Pentagonese, consisted of clotted groups of nouns, marching along in groups of three or four. Verbs, which connected nouns in purposive thrust, were regarded as unreliable and probably subversive. They talked too much, gave too much away.

Despite the Pentagon's best efforts, linguistically the Sixties were a noisy and exhilarating era. The Seventies gave us the argots of feminism and queerdom but then suddenly we were in the wastelands of Political Correctness, where non-white people were described as being "of color," cripples became "less-abled" and sexual preference (non-heterosexual) became LGBTQ, though another capital letter may have been added while my back was turned.

Where are we now? Irritating words and terms spread across the internet like plague through a European town in 1348. There's something very passive about the overall argot and a look through one's daily inbox is like walking along a beach piled with decayed words and terms. There's much more ill-written prose than there was thirty years ago.

¶ Discourse — This terrible word has been infecting the language for a generation at least. It has a pretentious timbre, lending factitious dignity to whoever happens to be holding the stage.

¶ "Massive" and its associate "whopping" — the only two words the left uses to indicate large numbers.

¶ This nomination landed in the email box from Francisco González.

> This is to congratulate you on your fantastic 'dung cart' section. Imagine how the manure from the 'tomberelles' gets translated, contaminating our Spanish language with the worst crop of bad English. On TV or the written press, we listen or read translated idiot propositions alien to our language, like 'all options on the table' — why on the table I ask, while the image of a retarded fool comes to my mind wanting to put food on his family- or 'the ball is on someone's court' while talking about life or death situations, peace or war if talking about nations, with the joy and relaxation of a ball game.
>
> Keep your excellent work coming, it does not matter that it will not be translated, like the regular dose of crap we get.
>
> From southeastern Spain, my best wishes to you and your great site. Cheers. Francisco González

¶ Thomas Naylor has had it with: "Have a nice one..."

> Nice what? Cheese, mushroom and pepperoni pizza? Hearty dump? Damn good f...? Well, you know. Probably the first — since most of those robotic sales types uttering that apogee of inanity have cheesey smiles on their faces and are programmed to masticate only sound-bite-sized slices.

¶ Neal Haiduck sends this:

> Dear Alex, there's surely room on the tumbril cart for "on" or "off" the table? I remember Obama saying that prosecuting Bush and Cheney were off the table.

> Obliterating Iran with nuclear devices is frequently an option that's on the table. Sincerely, Neal Haiduck

¶ Edward Wall offers a stringer of abused words:

> Not having the list, here are some of mine: "even as we speak," "terrorist" specially when uttered by supporters and officials of the empire and Israelis, "a class act," "quality" as in "quality player" good, bad, indifferent? "Community" this that and the other in a nation whose only "community" is in the Chamber of Commerce, "Issues," "athleticism," "defensing" and hundreds of others in any sports broadcast.

¶ The esteemable Bruce Anderson weighs in from Boonville:

> Hola, Alex. Not much in circulation yet but spotted twice now in edu-prose: … a search firm dedicated to SURFACING (my emphasis) appropriate candidates for school district leadership positions." I also nominate 'appropriate' as now applied to everything from mass murder to bad table manners. Best, Bruce at the AVA

Ed Szewczyk writes from Illinois:

> I have some nominations for the tumbrils: 1. "Robust," as in robust interrogation techniques, or robust Article II powers. Seems always to be used as a euphemism for the unconstitutional and/or violently illegal abuse of something… Ed Szewczyk, Granite City, IL

Troy Nichols proposes to dispose of an entire class of obnoxious business speech, including:

> the made-up business gerund (Examples: "decisioning," "bootstrapping," "costing," "tumbrilling?" New ones are being invented every day). These clunky mutations are often close to meaningless, and the rest of the world surely laughs when they hear us talking like that. At present these words are highly concentrated in corporate memos and various official statements, but they'll soon leak into the public discourse if left unchecked. You see it every once in a while already. Proliferation is certain. Let's preempt this danger and send them all to the tumbrils now. If there's any doubt about a certain word, say it in its infinitive form ("to decision," "to cost"). If it sounds ridiculous, off it goes...

¶ "The Other" made its long awaited appearance before the Revolutionary Tribunal presided over by Prosecutor Fouquier-Tinville. Popular feeling ran high on the grounds that "the Other" was actually a German spy operating under the cover name "Fichte," intent on undermining the Revolution by preaching divisiveness. "L'Autre à la lanterne!" was the vociferous popular chorus.

"The Other" made a poor impression in the hearing, standing in a posture of less than manly albeit slightly insolent submission and speaking mysteriously about "inter-subjectivity" but — perhaps fatally — also alluding to the "master-slave" relationship in a manner that displayed insufficient passion in denouncing the abominable practice of slavery, which ended in all French colonies the previous February, 1794.

"The Other" mustered a large number of character witness, ranging from the philosopher Hegel, to the psychoanalyst Lacan to writers Jean-Paul Sartre and Simone de Beauvoir, to Reason editor Jesse Walker (who defended "the Other" as having "an eldritch quality I like — academic jargon that feels Lovecraftian") to the literary critic Edward Said who spoke of the stigmatization of "the Other" in terms of what he described — to Prosecutor Fouquier-Tinville's visible bewilderment — as "Orientalism" and "western domination of the colonial subject." Prosecutor Fouquier-Tinville responded sharply that though the term "Orientalism" was unknown to him, he had long noted "the Other" as a subversive element in institutions of higher learning, sabotaging clear thought with "modish catchphrases long since drained of useful content." Fouquier-Tinville pointed sternly to recent successful prosecutions of "narrative" and "post-colonial."

The hearing was suspended to permit speedy trial of "nuanced," unanimously condemned to the guillotine by the jury.

¶ Now this, from CounterPuncher JoAnn Wypijewski:

> Sexual abuse is a term that ought to be summarily dispatched to the tumbrils, as it has lost any shred of meaning, which is the whole point in this extended night of moral panic. There is no need whatsoever for this term, except to obfuscate. There are plain terms, readily understood, with common meanings (or more common): rape, forced fellatio — strange, you never hear of forced cunnilingus — [Oh yes you do, see Jeffrey St Clair's recent essay on Willie Dixon, AC], exhibition-

ism, leering, groping, finger-fucking, pawing, dirty talk, kidnapping, exploitation in x, y and z ways (yes, that would require more words—how burdensome is precision), unwanted touching, unwanted hugging...

The list is long because people may experience, or claim to experience, different things as abuse. But abuse is potent in law, and is therefore a handmaid of prosecution. In the various sex panic stories over the past twenty years 'sexual abuse' has meant everything from fantasized Satanic black masses to actual rape to nudity in the YMCA showers. (That last is not a flourish; the Catholic Church caved, paying out tens of thousands of dollars to people who said they saw Father Geoghan walk around naked in the YMCA shower room, nothing else. He, as you recall, was murdered in prison to the cheers of the liberal faithful after he was convicted for touching a kid's ass while pulling him out of a pool.) Let's call things by their names. And let's restore 'fondling,' a word that has been yanked into the sexual abuse bag, to its proper place in the realm of sexual play. 'Molestation' is a fine word, and one no one would confuse with 'fondling.' Without the catch-all 'abuse,' people might be able to claw their way back to sanity by distinguishing what is harmless or unruly or actually criminal.

And while we're at it, let's throw sex offender into the tumbril. As it is, a sex offender might be: a rapist; a child who draws a stick figure with breasts and penis, a child who plays doctor with another or kisses another or slaps the ass of another or asks the teacher for a hug; a teacher who gives a hug; a voyeur; a collector of porn; a kidnapper and torturer; an exhibitionist; a person caught urinating in public; a high school senior who has sex with a high school freshman; anyone who transmits sexual pictures to another person; anyone who transmits pictures that some policeman decides are sexual to another person; anyone caught having sex in the bushes of a public park, etc. etc.

Like terrorist, 'sex offender' is most useful in defining a group of people out of the realm of rights, making them a new category of human being, against whom any atrocity of the state is considered acceptable.

> Exception: 'self-abuse,' which in its blur of rigor and humor is far more evocative of the act it describes than masturbation, onanism, self-pleasuring, jacking off, etc.

Thank you JoAnn. Prosecutor Fouquier-Tinville is giving the case his urgent attention.

¶ Speaking of the condemned, I'd never realized, until reading Neil Schaffer's biography, how close the Marquis de Sade came to being guillotined by the Committee of Public Safety.

His trial, which would also have been his death sentence followed by instant decapitation, was scheduled for July 27, 1794. But the bailiff never came for him at his prison at Picpus. There's no clear explanation why. Bribery of the bailiff by Sade's faithful friend Mme Quesnet may have been Sade's salvation. That same day, July 27, spelled Robespierre's own doom, on 9 Thermidor, in the revolutionary calendar. The next day Robespierre was executed and Sade was safe. He was freed on October 15, 1794. This was not the end of his experience in prison. By the end of 1801 Sade was in Charenton, dying there in 1814, his final liaison being with Magdeleine LeClerc, a 17-year-old. He was 74 and there seems to have been affection on both sides. He recorded her visits to the prison meticulously, as was his habit. The last embrace was their 94th.

Poor Mme de Sade. She had to run around Paris looking for glass test tubes that would serve as dildoes for her husband, the Marquis, to use in auto-erotic stimulation at his prison in Vincennes. She had to order them from a glass-blowing factory, where the sales folk would ogle respectable Renee, indicating their view that these glass flasks — Sade wanted some of them 9.5 inches in length — were intended for her own gratification. In 27 months, Sade noted, he used such flasks a total of 6,536 times, an average of eight a day.

Names Sade called his wife in one letter sent from Vincennes in the late fall of 1783: "Mohammed's delight," "heavenly pussy," "fresh pork of my thoughts," "shining paintbox of my eyes," "mirror of beauty," "spur of my nerves," "violet of the Garden of Eden," "seventeenth planet of space," "discharge of angelic spirit," "rose fallen from the bosom of Graces," "my baby doll."

¶ CounterPuncher Steve Leonard writes:

> They seem to be tighter than a congenital syndactylism: the vast majorities. I wonder if there are majorities vaster than vast, or what the vastest of the vast majori-

ties might look like? What about those majorities less than vast? Are they sub-vast or semi-vast or half-vast? Surely the vast majority of your readers will approve the tumbril ride for vast majority.

¶ This just in from Philip Bittenbender:

> Alex, speaking of time plans: Looking forward, it is now time to backtrack, reverse course, touch base, get on the same page, let bygones be bygones and then, regroup and move forward with best practices! Keep up the good work. Phil B.

Into the tumbrils with them. And while we're at it, let's toss in the last analysis, doomed to the same blade that dispatched the bottom line a few weeks ago.

¶ "Related to 'play by the rules,' justly guillotined a few weeks ago, is 'pay your fair share' — a demand from those who aren't paying their fair share for more from those they have already robbed. Eric Rosenbloom"

¶ "'Troubling' (Don't bother me with these grisly details). 'Concerned' (Ditto). Clancy Sigal."

¶ "Hi Alex, has Prosecutor Fouquier-Tinville done his due diligence on 'due diligence?' Bill Hatch."

¶ Since I cited the Marquis de Sade's narrow escape from the guillotine recently, several readers have urged that I remind CounterPunchers of the much better known escape of Tom Paine. Herewith, courtesy of Mark Scaramella, assistant editor of the great *Anderson Valley Advertiser*:

> Paine lived in France for most of the 1790s, becoming deeply involved in the French Revolution. He wrote the Rights of Man (1791) in part a defense of the French Revolution against its critics. His attacks on British writer Edmund Burke led to a trial and conviction in absentia in 1792 for the crime of seditious libel. In 1792, despite not speaking French, he was elected to the French National Convention. The Girondists regarded him as an ally. Consequently, the Montagnards, especially Robespierre, regarded him as an enemy. In December of 1793, he was arrested and imprisoned in Paris at the Bastille.

> Paine was set to be executed, but escaped it by some freaky chance. While in prison, Paine narrowly escaped execution. A guard walked through the prison placing a chalk mark on the doors of the prisoners who were due to be sent to the guillotine the next day. He placed a "4" on the door of Paine's cell, but Paine's door had been left open to let a breeze in, because Paine was seriously ill at the time. That night, his other three cellmates closed the door, thus hiding the mark inside the cell. The next day their cell was overlooked for the tumbril. "The Angel of Death" had passed over Paine. He kept his head and survived the few vital days needed to be spared by the fall of Robespierre (July 27, 1794).

¶ The *New York Times* continues to be disfigured by the "well" plague. Here is Jesse McKinley in the *NYT* in his piece "Whatever Happened to First Class?":

> This was the high life, I figured, a conviction that only intensified when the flight attendant approached with a silver tray and addressed me — unprompted — as 'Mr. McKinley.' Then he handed me, well, a towel. Or sort of.

Why did he hand him *well-a-towel*? Would not a simple towel have sufficed?

McKinley's piece, quite amusing on the topic of the low ebb to which first class seating on planes has now fallen, contained this marvelous bit of corporate-speak: "And those are just the perks on the plane. According to Fern Fernandez, managing director for marketing and customer loyalty of US Airways, for some customers they pale in comparison with the biggest prize of all: less time waiting to get on. 'Domestically, it's that ability to have an expedited experience in the boarding process,' he said. 'And having a little extra space.'"

The same *NYT* edition also featured Mark Bittman on Indian restaurants in London:

> But those that offer the real deal are amazing, and frankly have more guts than those that cater to, well, a white-tablecloth clientele.

Bringing up the rear was repeat offender Paul Krugman:

> Finally, there's Mr. Romney, who will probably get the nomination despite his evident failure to make an emotional connection with, well, anyone.

¶ Pepe Escobar of *Asia Times* sends this note:

> Dear Alex, I suggest the weaponized tumbrilization of 'international community' to the sound of David Bowie's Scary Monsters, Super Creeps. This is NOT a community, and—as a NATO/GCC compound—it couldn't be more provincial. And while we're at it, why not tumbrilize 'staunch ally' as well? All the best, Pepe/ Asia Times.

¶ CounterPunchers are a vigilant, dare I even say (a phrase under close scrutiny by Prosecutor Fouquier-Tinville) a blood-thirsty crowd. The Prosecutor's inbox is filled to overflowing with calls for revolutionary justice.

From Watsonville comes a denunciation from Frank Bardacke, who inexplicably quotes Carlyle, a fervent counter-revolutionary of course, but a stylist Frank has long admired:

> Like a black Spectre, daily at eventide, glides the Death-tumbril through the variegated throng of things.
>
> I accuse: privilege as a gerund. As in, "Privileging the body, he rarely missed a meal." Citoyen actif, Bardacke.

Yes indeed, Citoyen Bardacke. These gerunds are everywhere: gerund... girondin... I think the case is clear.

¶ From Gui Rochat, with the peremptory cry "Into the tumbril": 'Should,' a word too often used by progressives, reflecting de facto a redundant idealist and basically liberal compromise.'

¶ Shane Mayer presents a powerful case: "The Prosecutor will surely consider, for a brief but purposeful ride on the tumbril cart, the habit of converting punctuation marks into sentence fragments. The same sentiment used to be expressed with the equally imperious and unnecessary 'ipso facto': 'Smoking causes cancer. Period.' A quick and painless dispatching of the usage is just the thing; consider that it has already generated a staccato variation on its original theme: 'Smoking. Causes. Cancer. Period.'"

¶ Lawrence Magnuson draws an approving roar from the sans-culottes as he presses his j'accuse: "the tumbril, to fully do its stern duty, needs but one ecumenical occupant: 'unconscionable.' Was ever a more feckless state of the moral mind alluded to? Was ever outrage so easily negated? The blandest dead word I know."

¶ Sondjata Olatunji offers another object for annihilation: "Can we also put 'hyper-masculinity' on that cart? Each time I have heard the phrase I have asked the user to define 'normal masculinity' since there can be no ' hyper' or hypo' masculinity without some defined and accepted 'normal' masculinity."

"Normal masculinity" Sondjata? Now there's a can of worms.

¶ Each day, as the tumbrils creak towards the Place de la Revolution, one can see the pale faces of words and phrases seized by popular vigilance from the world of corporate language-mangling. CounterPuncher Pete Jones, who says he works in a place "inundated by verbal nonsense," advanced these candidates for the blade:

> To re-examine — to think about; to leverage — to use for future profit-making (why do they need a special word for this?); functional team — the group of coworkers you work with on a daily basis; iterative thinker — someone who is indecisive, a trait which appears to no longer be a flaw; bandwidth — this is the most stupefying of all, as it is constantly used, knowingly — with an implied wink, occasionally — for the simpler, but unspeakable term, 'free time.'

The jury had no difficulty in imposing the supreme penalty.

¶ Unctuous. It's standard in pretentious food reviews, as in "unctuous sauce," though not "unctuous head waiter" where the usage would be permissible once or twice a year. Into the cart with it, shoulder to shoulder with "vibrant," denounced to Prosecutor Fouquier-Tinville by Rick Claymore, who writes, "I've been over this one for decades, but, living in the Bay Area, where every event or place is 'vibrant,' I cannot escape."

Rick also wants to consign "old school" to the tumbrils. "I'm sick to death of hearing anything older than 1980 being referred to as, 'old school.' I was recently informed that my crocheted bicycle gloves are, 'old school.'" I'm not so sure about this. "Old-school" is usually linked with "courtesy" or some kindred trait of times long gone. But I tremble for its future once Prosecutor Fouquier-Tinville catches sight of the word.

¶ It's time to throw "noted" into the tumbril. Article after article, I read that X "noted" and then Y "noted" and then Z "noted." In the old days we took more trouble. Our sources and authorities "pointed out" or "stressed" or "hinted" or "explained" or sometimes simply just "said." We rang the changes. Now it's just one single noted and it's got to stop, with a summary thwock and a cackle from the tricoteuses.

¶ Following "noted" up onto the scaffold will be "penned." Even though fountain pens, let alone quills, are as rare as tumbrils, I read more than I should of people "penning" an article, or sometimes "authoring" it, which is nearly as bad. What's wrong with "wrote?"

¶ Richard Kidd writes from Winnipeg: "I would like to nominate two of President Obama's favorite expressions. 'Let me be clear,' or more commonly, 'Let me be perfectly clear.' If you want to be clear, then phrase your ideas clearly. 'Make no mistake...' I suppose this qualifier is intended to warn listeners against misinterpretation, or perhaps against doubting the sincerity of the speaker. It's another of Obama's annoying catch phrases that richly deserves tumbrilization."

¶ And from long-term CounterPuncher Glenn Ierley:

> Years ago, Edwin Newman inveighed in vain against the then common custom of commencing observations with the pointless interrogatory phrase 'You know something?' For want of a tumbril this phrase died a few years later of natural causes, but not before spreading its mutant spores.
>
> The recently hatched spawn of this is another pointless interrogatory phrase now appended to all too many observations, as I was reminded on seeing it occur not once, but twice, in a column by that fearless defender of the status quo, George Will. The offender? 'Who knew?'
>
> You know something? Ask not for whom the tumbril rolls, it rolls for thee. Who knew? Best, Glenn.

I say Aye to these. Prosecutor Fouquier-Tinville will give the charges his usual scrupulous attention.

¶ Rumors had been sweeping the Revolutionary Tribunal that prosecutor Fouquier-Tinville would be handing down an important indictment. In the event it turned out to be a powerful one from *CounterPunch* co-editor Jeffrey St Clair, author of important works on the environment and on "green" hokum, and a known admirer of Maximilien Robespierre and his associate Saint-Just. Let us give Citoyen actif Jeffrey the floor without further ado:

> The environmental movement has become freighted with more and more deceptive terms. Let's begin by banishing the tiresome phrase sustainable development. Coined by NGOs in the 1970s, this discreditable term has been used to put a green gloss on everything from mega-dams to rainforest logging. Endless development is a more accurate description.
>
> Next, let us eliminate the Mephistophelian phrase win-win solution, a verbal potion of the Clinton era that was used to justify oil drilling in the Arctic, logging in the redwoods, and rollbacks in air pollution standards. In win-win solutions, industry gets what it wants and environmental groups get paid in grants to go along with the deal.
>
> Finally, let us jettison the term holistic, especially when affixed to "ecosystem" or "resource management." "Holistic is a merely a New Age-update of the venerable term "multiple-use," one of the oldest cons in the history of conservation. Multiple-use was the ludicrous notion that public lands could be all things to all people (or more properly all industries). In other words, wildlife could peacefully co-exist with mining, logging, livestock and off-road vehicle use. Holistic ecosystem management posits the same battered notion, but escalates the deception by suggesting that logging and grazing are actually beneficial to the long-term health of the ecosystem.

The revolutionary tribunal's jury did not tarry in issuing its summary verdict. Off rattled the tumbril and soon, after "win-win" had been politely prised apart by Executioner Sanson, the fatal blade rose and fell.

Also consigned to the tumbril, the portmanteau term strategist, meaning anyone invoked by a political journalist as a source.

¶ "Alex, here are a couple of related nominations: the repugnant 'walk back,' and its passive, reflexive, regurgitive form 'I mis-spoke myself.' Cheers, Marv Waterstone."

¶ In the dock is "anecdotal," long sought by the force of revolutionary vigilance. Prosecutor Fouquier-Tinville says he can do no better than read from the denunciation filed with his office by citoyen actif, Patrick Cockburn:

> A telling example of how undervaluing evidence as 'anecdotal' gives a free pass to misrepresentation, fraud and crime came last week in a report in Britain over unsafe breast implants. It had emerged that 47,000 British women had French manufactured implants made out of mattress gel using industrial grade silicon, never intended for medical use, that can burst and swell in the body. The 'deliberate fraud' by the French company was unmasked by French investigators in 2010. In Britain, it emerged, surgeons had warned that the implants were rupturing during demonstrations as long ago as 2006, one demanding the implants no longer be used. Two other surgeons had experience of the 'catastrophic disintegration' of implants. But the British government medical devices watchdog, MHRA, decided to do nothing because. so the report says, the evidence was 'anecdotal.' Furthermore the official watchdog, discounting the evidence of three surgeons, felt that to issue a warning would lead to an 'unwanted scare which could have serious commercial implications.'

There were lively outbursts of emotion during the unfolding of this outrage to morals and upright conduct and it was clear to "anecdotal" in the dock that this was not its lucky day and that a rendez-vous with the fatal blade would not be long postponed. Sentence was duly pronounced, without a single dissenting voice.

¶ This just in from Michael Dawson up in Portland, Oregon:

> More on 'in harm's way': This one was apparently used by our friend Staff Sgt. Robert Bales in a 2009 Pentagon-published discourse on how to distinguish 'good guys' from 'bad guys': 'We discriminated between the bad guys and the noncombatants, and then afterward we ended up helping the people that three or four hours before were trying to kill us. I think that's the real difference between being an American as opposed to

> being a bad guy, someone who puts his family in harm's way like that.'
>
> In harm's way. It dehumanizes and dehistoricizes all enemies. It flatters the speaker as somebody who chooses to stop Evil, presumably also suggesting the notion that, once one gains that status, one has the right to go shoot up a village. J'accuse.

¶ Now up in front of the revolutionary tribunal: "this is not who we are," the denunciation lodged by Geoff Gray:

> From Obama after the Bales butchery in Afghanistan: 'The killing of innocent civilians is outrageous and it's unacceptable. It's not who we are as a country, and it does not represent our military.' On why Obama wouldn't release photos of the dead Bin Laden: 'We don't need to spike the football…that's not who we are.' From Hillary at the UN, post Bales: 'We send our condolences to families who have lost their loved ones and to the people of Afghanistan…This is not who we are.' Another from Hillary commenting on the behavior of the audience at the Republican debate that booed a gay soldier: 'That's not reflective of who we are.'

Phrase duly condemned and dispatched to the implacable blade.

¶ Clancy Sigal, citoyen actif, hales a worthy duo in front of the tribunal: "arguably" and "hardscrabble." There's a roar of approval from the sans-culottes, as prosecutor Fouquier-Tinville demolishes a rambling speech of self-exculpation from "arguably." Hardscrabble is already half dead from overuse, even before sentence is pronounced and carried out.

¶ From Helmut Wallenfels comes a plump candidate for the tumbril: existential threat: "This phrase is guilty of the capital crimes of pretentiousness, pomposity and trying to hitch a free ride on the coat tails of Heidegger, Sartre and Camus."

¶ Finally, a plea for summary justice from Lester Shepherd of Roanoke, Alabama: "oeuvre: No normal person can spell it, no normal person can pronounce it and it is surely, solely, used to impress." Fouquier-Tinville, scrupulous as ever in his fairness, says the case needs further investigation.

¶ The common view is that thousands of French aristos perished under the blade. Not true. Greer's statistical study, *The Incidence of the Terror,* published in 1935, shows that 666 nobles got the chop in Paris and another 1,543 in the rest of France. Compare that to the carnage after the French commune of 1871 when some 20,000 Communards were executed.

The best defense of the French Revolution and its supposed excesses is surely that of Mark Twain in *A Connecticut Yankee*:

> There were two 'Reigns of Terror' if we would remember it and consider it; the one wrought murder in hot passion, the other in heartless cold blood; the one lasted mere months, the other had lasted a thousand years; the one inflicted death upon ten thousand persons, the other upon a hundred millions; but our shudders are all for the 'horrors' of the minor Terror, the momentary Terror, so to speak; whereas, what is the horror of swift death by the axe, compared with lifelong death from hunger, cold, insult, cruelty and heart-break? What is swift death by lightning compared with death by slow fire at the stake? A city cemetery could contain the coffins filled by that brief Terror which we have all been so diligently taught to shiver at and mourn over; but all France could hardly contain the coffins filled by that older and real Terror; that unspeakably bitter and awful Terror which none of us have been taught to see in its vastness or pity as it deserves.

Almost all the executions were performed by the public executioner, Charles-Henri Sanson, the rest by his sons, one of whom — Gabriel — perished by slipping off the scaffold.

¶ A slow week on the verbal front. "Has 'infotainment' been judged and sentenced yet?" asks John Sprey. "I heard it used in a car ad the other day, something along the lines of 'cutting edge infotainment system.' Maybe 'cutting edge' could go too?"

¶ Carol Fitzmaurice, in a hand-written denunciation, calls on revolutionary justice for "sort of," and "kind of." Prosecutor Fouquier-Tinville has added the denunciations to his stack.

¶ Fouquier-Tinville is preparing for a major trial, having announced the arrest and incarceration in the Conciergerie of "speaking truth to power"— a hugely annoying phrase, simultaneously exaggerating the courage required to tell the truth and underestimating power's own resourcefulness in adjusting truth to its own requirements. As Fouquier-Tinville tartly remarked, is the implication that the Revolutionary Tribunal does not want to know the truth?

As Louis Patrick writes from Memphis:

> Speaking truth to power. What a ridiculous joke that has always been. What is power if not the ability to create the truth by which the rest of us must live? The elite have never been Christ-like fools wandering blindly in a moral wilderness, waiting only to be awakened by the enlightened. They are predators. Murder and lies are mother's milk.

¶ And from Missy Beattie these little ones to toss into Fouquier-Tinville's in-tray: kind of, sort of, like sort of, and kind of, kinda, sorta. Last week there were calls for a couple of these to take the final ride. The people's vigilance has clearly been aroused.

¶ Here's a note from the sensible Bill Allen of Philo:

> Alex, during last week's tumbril break, while the blade was re-sharpened and the cart wheels greased, Fouquier-Tinville's agents — ever vigilant — fingered another enemy of the revolution, an expression that has managed to evade tribunal scrutiny and a well-deserved turn in the tumbril: the new normal.
>
> "The new normal" is the new vexing news-speak for matters that are rotten. Mark how "the new normal" only refers to degeneration and deterioration — political, economic, social, cultural, environmental, and so on.
>
> That our kids are graduating from college with no job prospects and debts approaching a home mortgage is the new normal.
>
> That millions of skilled factory workers and tradespeople can only find work flipping burgers or emptying bedpans in nursing homes is the new normal.
>
> That the NSA now vacuums up and stores all of our electronic communications is the new normal.
>
> That grannies and toddlers are 'groped or scoped' at airports is the new normal.
>
> That our legal system has become two-tiered — no accountability for political and economic elites while the rest of us face strip searches and isolation cells for petty infractions — is the new normal.

> Perhaps I missed one, but I can't recall any usage of 'the new normal' in reference to a situation that is better now than it was a decade or a generation ago — unless it was used in a corporate board room.
>
> Those NPR newscasters and mainstream writers who like to use the term think they are being savvy. Actually, they are wittingly or unwittingly spreading establishment propaganda like crap off the back of a tumbril. 'The new normal' implies the citizenry must passively accept and become adjusted to whatever unfavorable or oppressive conditions our dominant institutions (plus market forces) have created.
>
> If I may reword a statement by the late philosopher and teacher J. Krishnamurti: There's nothing 'normal' about being well adjusted to a sick society. Off with it! Best regards, Bill Allen, Philo, CA.

Bill, your denunciation carries no small measure of the passion of the great Maximilien. The "new normal" has trundled on its last journey to the Place de la Revolution, shoulder to shoulder with "nuanced," a wormy little term that has crept into popular usage in the press in recent months. Its function seems to be one of flattery by the writer for sentiments which, if set down in straightforward English, would excite derision, as in "In his nuanced arguments for reforms in Social Security and Medicare…"

¶ My brother Patrick sagely observes:

> In the wake of the Hollande victory there may be excessive demand for tumbrils in Paris to cope with those partisans of the Sarkozy regime unwise enough to delay too long their flight across the Rhine or to the Channel ports. This is a frustrating time, of course, for Fouquier-Tinville, wishing to push ahead with his good work, but perhaps a moment also for reflection and even a more "nuanced" approach on his part. For instance were all those condemned in the past equally guilty? The phrase "bottom line" is overused, but is there an alternative carrying the same meaning? "Please come to a conclusion" sounds too starchy and dull, "Get on with it" too rude… Perhaps there should be a separate category of words and phrases in danger of the fatal blade but might still be saved. There is "nuanced," as used above, which was a perfectly good word until journalists started using

> it to suggest (with a slight touch of self-preening) that there might be more than one reason why something is happening. "Remnants" had been doing no harm until it was used in phrases like "the remnants of Saddam Hussein's regime" or "al-Qa'ida remnants" to explain why people whom Washington had claimed were dead and buried still seemed to be in business. For F-T, surely, not just a challenge but an opportunity.

¶ Domenic Maltempi requests that "stand idly by" be brought to revolutionary justice. It's true that the phrase is often to be found in speeches that also say "all options are on the table." (Summarily guillotined a while ago.) Prosecutor Fouquier-Tinville made a fine speech pouring ridicule on the absurdity, nay the counter-revolutionary import of the phrase. So off goes "stand idly by" to the Place de La Revolution.

¶ With rare emotion Prosecutor Fouquier-Tinville announced that "play by the rules" had been captured by revolutionary vigilance, and faced the supreme penalty. This pious phrase, he said, is the tribute power pays to the oppressed. Yes, he cried, the feudal peasants whose daughters were raped by Monsieur Le Vicomte "played by the rules," even as they groaned under extra taxes levied by the Vicomte. "Our glorious revolution says No, we do not play by the rules." A stormy ovation accompanied the condemned to his final night in the Conciergerie.

¶ The keen blade of justice must fall swiftly on the word "tsunami" which has turned into a cliché through over use with astonishing speed. This happened rapidly after the 2004 Indian Ocean Tsunami and its use reached epidemic proportions after the Tsunami in Japan in 2011. Its use is mainly to add verbal spice and drama to usually mundane events by suggesting that what is happening is massive, devastating and unstoppable.

Users of the word can often hope to see their use of the phrase "a tsunami of...." promoted into a headline. For instance, take the case of identity theft tax fraud in southern Florida. Whatever else this is doing it is not, unlike Sri Lanka in 2004 or Fukushima in 2011, killing a lot of people. But the chief federal prosecutor for the Southern District of Florida, Wilfredo A. Ferrer, first described it as an "epidemic" and then added, "The I.R.S. is doing what they can to prevent this, but this is like a tsunami of fraud."

And sure enough "tsunami of fraud" was in the headline in the *International Herald Tribune* version of the *New York Times* story. Another charge lodged by citoyen actif Patrick Cockburn.

¶ And finally this urgent indictment from my brother Andrew Cockburn: "I must denounce 'contrarian' to the prosecutor. A stupid label, implying an opportunist lack of principle thereby facilitating others to dismiss those so named without need to distinguish between real and fake convictions. Space should be found on the tumbril for anyone who applies that label to themselves, thereby glorying in their own lack of conviction."

The verdict was swiftly announced and the merciless blade has already fallen. May they repose in eternal silence.

The condemned

Sustainable

Iconic

Narrative

Parse

Meme

Gamechanger

Expensed

Leveraged

Project

Conversation

National conversation

Chattering classes

Governance

If you will

It's the economy, stupid, and variants

Well

Er

Staunch

At the end of the day

Fat lady sings

Rubber meets the road

Bad guys

Really

Just sayin'

Stakeholder

Folks

Grow

Blood and treasure

In harm's way

Reaching out

Unpack

Excavate

Closure

Bottom line

Discourse

Massive

Whopping

All options on the table

Even as we speak

Class act

Defensing

Surfacing

Appropriate

Robust

Decisioning

Bootstrapping

Costing

The Other

Nuanced

Sexual abuse

Looking forward

Backtrack

Sex offender

Vast majority

Reverse course

Touch base
On the same page
In the last analysis
Regroup
Play by the rules
Pay your fair share
Troubling
Concerned
International community
Privileging
Should
Ipso facto
Period
Unconscionable
Hyper-masculinity
Re-examine
Functional team
Iterative thinker
Bandwidth
Free time
Unctuous
Vibrant
Old school
Noted
Penned
Let me be clear
You know something
Who knew
Sustainable development
Win-win solution

Holistic
Strategist
Walk back
Mis-spoke
This is not who we are
Arguably
Hardscrabble
Existential threat
Oeuvre
Infotainment
Cutting edge
Sort of, (and its variants)
Kind of, (and its variants)
Speaking truth to power
New normal
Remnants
Anecdotal
Stand idly by
Tsunami
Contrarian

Citoyans Actif

Fred Gardner
Jon Swift
Wat Stearns
Leslie Cockburn
Jean-Pierre Duboucheron
Sean Dunne
Vukoni Lupa-Lasaga
Egido Mondolfi
Natalie Bauman
Joe Paff
Karen Paff
Michael Greenberg
Jack Flannigan
Jeremy Pikser
Kevin Rath
Patrick Cockburn
Dennis Chericone
James Blum
Richard Stack
Doug Lummis
Francisco Gonzalez
Thomas Naylor
Neal Haiduck
Edward Wall
Bruce Anderson
Ed Szewcyk
Troy Nichols
JoAnn Wypijewski
Steve Leonard
Philip Bittenbender
Clancy Sigal
Eric Rosenbloom
Bill Hatch
Mark Scaramella
Pepe Escobar
Frank Bardacke
Gui Rochat
Shane Mayer
Lawrence Magnuson
Sondata Olatunji
Pete Jones
Rick Claymore
Richard Kidd
Glenn Ierley
Jeffrey St. Clair
Marv Waterstone
Geoff Gray
Helmut Wallenfels
Lester Shepherd
John Sprey
Lewis Patrick
Missy Beattie
William Allen
Domenic Maltempi
Andrew Cockburn